T0370505

They Said I Couldn't, But Yes I Can!

Written By
Marva Bourne

Illustrated By
Candice Bourne Enang

AuthorHouse™
1663 Liberty Drive
Bloomington, IN 47403
www.authorhouse.com
Phone: 1 (800) 839-8640

Published by AuthorHouse 12/14/2018

ISBN: 978-1-5462-4438-7 (sc)
ISBN: 978-1-5462-4439-4 (e)

Library of Congress Control Number: 2018907339

Print information available on the last page.

Dedication

For Xavier, Mel, Havilyn (Uyai) and all the other children who dream, will grow up to be great, and will inspire greatness.

Simone Biles

2016 Olympic Gymnast

1

It takes a village.
A statement quite true,
and that's what my family
decided to do.
I had many challenges,
but continued to dream.
The tougher my trials,
though hopeless they seem,
only prepared me for life's balance beam.

Simone Biles is the first African-American World All-Round Champion. She earned four gold medals and one bronze medal at the Rio Olympics, 2016.

Charles Bolden
Administrator of NASA and NASA Astronaut

As a child I watched the stars at night
and marveled at the awesome sight.
I'd rest my hand upon my face
and wonder at what lies in space.
Wished I could go beyond the stars,
maybe even land on Mars.
Messages that I couldn't
attacked from every side,
but I fought them back with, "Yes I can,"
and swelled my chest with pride.
Now a veteran of four space flights.
I still wonder at the stars at nights.

Charles F. Bolden, Jr. is the first
African-American to be appointed
Administrator of NASA.

Mike Carey
Super Bowl XLII Referee

I played for college as a running back.
Fought challenges just 'cause I was Black.
So much criticism after each game.
Many attempted to smear my name.
They said I couldn't,
but they were dead wrong.
To referee Giants, I had to be strong.

Mike Carey was designated as referee of Super Bowl XLII between the New England Patriots and New York Giants, becoming the first African-American referee to receive the prestigious assignment.

Michelle Carter
2016 Olympic Shot Putter

I was built to do something.
That, I surely know.
Every muscle and fiber,
from my head to my toe.
They said I couldn't,
"It hadn't been done of late.
Not since the bronze in forty-eight."
But, I placed the shot put to my ear,
focused on what I know.
Then gained the gold and their respect,
as I gave the final throw.

Michelle Carter won the 2016 gold medal at the Rio Olympics on the last of her six throws. She is the first African-American woman to win a gold medal in the field of shot put.

Ta-Nehisi Coates
Author, Journalist, Educator and Comic Book Writer

I show how slavery and segregation
prevent us from attaining wealth.
How police brutality and aggravation,
affect self-esteem and mental health.
Men must not be measured
by our levels of melanin,
but we should all be treasured,
despite the color of our skin.
They said I couldn't,
but I sure could,
write a story that was super good.

Ta-Nehisi Coates' article "Reparation" was awarded the George Polk Award for commentary.

Misty Copeland
Principal Ballet Dancer

My early years were marred
with battles and contention.
Introduction to ballet
was a timely intervention.
They said that I couldn't,
I didn't stand a chance,
but I changed those words to "Yes I can,"
and now outshine in dance.

Misty Copeland is the first
African-American woman to be
named Principal Dancer in the
75-year history of American
Ballet Theater.

Shani Davis

2006 Olympic Speed Skater

My success came at great sacrifice.
No skater can catch me on the ice.
They said I couldn't,
but I surely did.
My speed skating skills cannot be hid.
I followed my dreams.
Now look at me,
breaking records for all to see.

Shani Davis became World Champion for the fourth time in 2014-2015 Winter Olympics.

Viola Davis
Actress and Producer

The only thing that holds us back is opportunity.
Upon reflection I now thank my life of poverty.
It sharpened my imagination,
and set my acting skills in motion.
They said I couldn't,
that I didn't have the look,
but when opportunity came,
that's the chance I took.

Viola Davis is the first African-American woman to win an Emmy Award for "Outstanding Actress" in a Drama Series.

Ava DuVernay
**Film Director, Producer, Screen Writer and
Distributor of Independent Film**

As a young girl I would imagine…
If I were homeless where would I sleep,
under a bridge or a hillside so steep?
If I were in prison what would I miss?
Slavery still happens, I would like to change this.
"It can't be done!" was shouted at me.
I began to read and started to see.
Whites in America, many seem to lack
true understanding of what it is to be Black.
My movies have begun to enlighten,
about racial injustice and slavery in prison.

 First African-American woman to be nominated for best director by the Golden Globe Awards for Selma.

Geoffrey S. Fletcher
Screenwriter, film director, and adjunct film professor

It started when I was a boy,
with a video camera and favorite toy.
I had a wild imagination,
created movies with such passion.
Could one with such a humble start
cause men to marvel at his art?
They said I couldn't,
they had a feeling,
I couldn't get past the glass ceiling.
Ten long years but I didn't rest,
until my movie was the best.

Geoffrey S. Fletcher is the first African-American to win an Academy Award in writing. He won for Best Adapted Screenplay for "Precious."

Haben Girma
**Deafblind Graduate of Harvard Law School
and Disability Rights Advocate**

They said I couldn't,
"It was an impossibility."
Born deaf and blind,
how could I hear or see?
The odds were all against me;
immigrant, Black, minority,
female with disabilities.
But if Helen Keller did it
without technology,
I could go much further,
with new opportunities.
Now a Harvard Law School graduate,
first student deaf and unable to see.
I champion and I advocate for others just like me.

In 2015, Haben Girma was named a White House Champion of Change and was also appointed to the national board of trustees for the Helen Keller Services for the Blind.

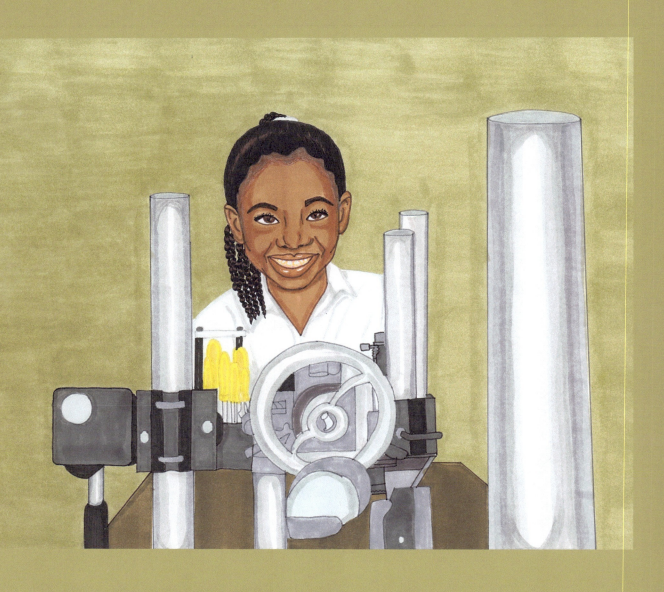

Hadiyah-Nicole Green
Medical Physicist

Orphaned while still very young,
aunt and uncle raised me strong.
Do not settle like the rest,
work real hard and do your best.
They said that I couldn't ever,
find the answer to fighting cancer.
I refused to listen to that claim.
Now, the world will know my name.

Hadiyah-Nicole Green won a $1.1 million grant to develop a laser that kills cancer cells.

Hill Harper
Actor and Author

Brilliant and good looking too.
I always knew what I wanted to do.
They said I couldn't,
"Black men don't succeed in school,
they mess around and play the fool."
I challenged their perception of the Black Man.
Was part of the movement "Yes We Can."
Author and "Outstanding Actor" awarded to me.
Now, helping brothers be the best they can be.

 Hill Harper won the NAACP Image Award for Outstanding Actor in a Drama Series for three consecutive years (2008–2010) for his portrayal of Dr. Sheldon Hawkes on CSI: NY.

Michelle Howard
United States Navy Officer

Dreams to serve my country
began so very early.
They said that I couldn't,
gender was my problem,
"Four-star generals were not meant for women."
Especially, ones with the color of my skin.
Just a touch too much of melanin.
But nothing could stop my high ambition.
Laws were changed to allow us admission.
Now, I am the first woman in the military
to command a combat ship on the sea.

Michelle J. Howard is the first woman to become a four-star admiral, and first African-American woman to command a Navy ship, the USS Rushmore.

Eric Holder
82nd Attorney General of the United States and Lawyer

Attorney General number eighty-two,
that's the job I had to do.
I felt we can and must ensure,
that Americans remain secure.
They said I couldn't,
"This position no Blacks can achieve."
But tough jobs call for toughness,
I'm sure you will agree.
Obama appointed the toughest.
That's what he saw in me.

 Eric Holder is the first African-American to be appointed Attorney General of the United States.

Barrington Irving
Aviator

With many obstacles all around,
I ascended high above the ground.
In my heart I dared to dream
to be the best they'd ever seen.
They said I couldn't,
"I must be insane.
Could a pilot fly without a plane?"
I accepted the challenge,
I thought it was cool.
Now, I teach flying classes in school.

In 2007, at age 23, Barrington Irving became the youngest pilot to fly solo around the world in a single-engine airplane. He flew the plane "Inspiration" around the world in 96 days 150 hours.

Shawna Rochelle Kimbrell
Fighter Pilot and Lieutenant Colonel in the United States Air Force

As a child I dared to dream
that one day I would soar.
Education was the valued key,
that could open any door.
They said that I couldn't,
"Didn't have what it took."
I knew that was nonsense.
Kept my nose in every book.
Did not have a second plan.
Desired no other things
than to be a combat pilot,
and now I've earned my wings.

Shawna Rochelle Kimbrell is the first African-American woman combat pilot in the United States Air Force.

Norm Lewis

Actor and Baritone Singer

Make-up and costume then off I go.
Starring as the Phantom in a Broadway show.
How did such fortune smile at me?
An opportunity for the world to see.
They said I couldn't, "Never on Broadway."
Now, I hide a smile behind the mask
that once was a forbidden task.
I take a long bow at curtain call,
and think of my brothers as I stand real tall.

 Norm Lewis is the first African-American to play the part of the Phantom in "The Phantom of the Opera" on Broadway.

Simone Manuel
2016 Olympic Competition Swimmer

"She defied the odds at winning."
This was said about my swimming.
They said I couldn't make the score.
Never was this done before.
An African-American female swimmer.
Won four medals: Two gold, two silver.
Practiced hard and stayed in school.
Now, breaking records in the pool.

 Simone Manuel is the first African-American woman to win a gold medal in the individual Olympic swimming category.

Barack Obama
44th President of the Unites States

Dad black as pitch.
Mom white as snow.
Two cultures within me
wherever I go.
They said that I couldn't,
"That I didn't dare,
fight for affordable health care."
I believe in the words "Yes We Can,"
that brought change for every American.
I did my best with much opposition,
to restore some hope to our tired nation.

 Barack Obama became the first
African-American President of the
United States of America.

Michelle Obama
**Lawyer, University Administrator, Writer and
former First Lady of the United States**

They said I couldn't,
"Set my sights too high.
Shouldn't gaze upon the sky."
Descendant of a slave.
I had to be brave.
I push for higher education;
For healthy families to stay in motion;
Letting adversity and negativity
become fuel for their energy.
Most educated and fashion savvy.
America's First Lady,
that was my destiny.

Michelle Obama is the first African-American First Lady and first First Lady to have earned two graduate degrees.

Tyler Perry
Actor, Playwright, Filmmaker and Comedian

Bullying and fighting with family and friends
caused me to think of very sad ends.
"They said I couldn't,
You're not very smart,
not good at language art,
you ought to know better."
But, my career began by writing one letter.
They said, "You'll never succeed without a degree."
Now, my movies and plays many flock to see.

 Tyler Perry is the first African-American to launch his own film and television studio.

Claressa Shields
Professional Boxer

The smile on my face was natural you know,
after winning a gold medal twice in a row.
Of course they thought I couldn't
do something so grand.
So much going against me,
how could I still stand?
Thanks to my family
they helped me to see.
Gender doesn't matter,
it's the drive inside of me.

Clarissa Shields is the first African-American woman to win a boxing gold medal. She is the first African-American boxer, male or female, to win an Olympic title twice in a row.

Bryan Stevenson
Lawyer, Social Justice Activist, Founder and Executive Director of the Equal Justice Initiative and Clinical Professor

My life is totally dedicated
to help the innocent and poor.
Death row inmates and even children,
forgotten behind the prison door.
They said I couldn't,
but I sure can,
fight for justice for my fellow man.
Freeing many from incarceration
to enjoy a life of full redemption.

 Bryan Stevenson won the Mac Arthur "Genius" Grant. He was awarded two honorary doctor's degrees: One from the University of Delaware and one from Williams College for his contribution to society.

Ciara Taylor
**Founding Member, Political Director and the Director
of Political Consciousness at Dream Defenders**

People told me I couldn't do it,
but I prove them wrong every minute.
By changing laws like "Stand your ground,"
which are designed to keep us down.
Harnessing the power of the young
to stand for right and challenge wrong.
The world needs people brave like me
to fight for justice and equality.

Ciara Taylor became the Political Director of Dream Defenders: A human rights organization.

Jasmine Twitty
Associate Judge for the Easley South Carolina Municipal Court

I followed my vision with intention
keeping sight upon my goal.
They said I couldn't,
but I didn't listen,
the drive was deep within my soul.
I never see the glass half empty,
I always see the half that's full.
Reminded myself that I'm worthy.
Now, sisters behind me I can pull.

Jasmine Twitty was the youngest
person to be sworn in as a judge
in Easley, South Carolina.

Kara Walker
**Contemporary Painter, Sillouettist, Print-maker,
Installation Artist and Filmmaker**

I create pictures that tell a story.
Dreaming up paintings led to my glory.
Black paper silhouettes led to my fame.
Many people now know my name.
My work was shown at the Drawing Center,
addressing issues like race and gender.
My critics said I didn't dare.
I proved to them I didn't care.

In 2007, Kara Walker was listed among Time Magazine's 100 Most Influential People in The World.

In 2012, she was elected to the American Academy of Arts and Sciences.

Venus and Serena Williams
Professional Tennis Players, 2000/2008/2012
Olympic Doubles and Grand Slam Winners

It started as a seed of hope
within our father's chest,
that his two girls would one day
be the finest and the best.
They tried to say we couldn't,
"Tennis is not your game.
Black girls out of Compton,
don't stand a chance at fame."
Who would have thought
without the "right" looks,
these two girls out of Compton,
would be in history books.

Venus and Serena Williams are the first African-American doubles team to be named year-end world champions by the International Tennis Federation.